ARE YOU SUITED...
AND READY FOR BATTLE?

Ephesians 6:10-18

EVERY BELIEVER'S GUIDE

TO

SPIRITUAL WARFARE

Karen D. Carver-Prater

Are you Suited and Ready for Battle?

Every Believers Guide to Spiritual Warfare
Copyright © March 2021 by Karen D. Carver-Prater
Published in the United States of America by
Gospel 4 U Network

www.gospel4unetwork.com

All rights reserved. No part of this book may be reproduced or transmitted in anyway by means, electronic, mechanical, photocopy, recording or otherwise, without prior permission of the author except as provided by USA copyright law.

Scriptures are taken from the
Holy Bible, the King James Version (KJV)
unless otherwise marked.
ISBN: 978-0-692-63086-0
Printed in United States of America

March 2021

TABLE OF CONTENTS

Acknowledgements	v
Dedication	vii
Foreword	ix
Introduction	xi
What Is Spiritual Warfare?	xiii
Introduction	1
Satan's Strategies	5
Personal Encounter With Spiritual Warfare	13
Different Pieces Of The Armor	16
Purpose Of Individual Pieces Of The Armor	19
"The Belt Of Truth - Psalm 51:6"	20
"Breastplate Of Righteousness"	28
Feet Shod with the Preparation of the Gospel of Peace	40
Shield of Faith	43
Helmet of Salvation	46
Renewing the mind	49
Sword of the Spirit (Word of God)	51
Praying Always (1 Thessalonians 5:17)	54

Acknowledgements

This book was started many years before the actual publishing. I am realizing now that it had to start when it did and that it could not be completed until now but that the things I experienced in the years between were needed in order to complete it at this appointed time.

I thank God for His awesome timing, love and patience that He has shown me over the years of my life. Without a doubt, this would not have even been remotely possible without the guidance of His loving hand. Forever I will follow Him!

I'd like to acknowledge my earthly help; To Steven, my husband and partner of ten years, I thank you for patiently reading early drafts of the manuscript which is now this book! You were right, as long as I trusted God, it would get done in His timing. Thank you so much for your encouraging words as I labored over this piece of work. I love you and appreciate everything you have contributed. I'd like to thank Gospel 4u publishing team for such attention to detail, with a special thanks to Joanna Ottey Birchett who worked so diligently to bring my book, my dream to life, the professionalism of Gospel4u is second to none. Thank you to a special friend and author in her own right Pastor Veronica Dixon,

Founder of *"She Blossoms By Being R.E.A.L"*, thank you for all of your prayers and being a cheerleader from the sidelines. Last but definitely not least, thank you to Claressa Elliott likewise a friend who I like to refer to as an "unlikely ally", a spiritual diamond in the rough who will touch many lives for the Lord in this battle called "Spiritual Warfare", thank you for your encouragement and prayers in this journey. This list of acknowledgements is in no way exhaustive, there are many, many more who have had a part, you know who you are and I love you ALL! God bless you all!

Dedication

To my sister Reverend Dr. Patricia A. Efiom who when I had moments of self doubt has always been an encourager to me in my endeavors and reminded me *"You are a woman who has the hand of God on her life, walk in your authority..."*. Last but definitely not least, to the reader who has picked up this book and will be strengthened by the words penned here, though we may never meet, I take this time to thank you. You have my word, when you finish reading this book you *will* be able to say with confidence, *"I am now Suited and Ready for Battle"*

Foreword

Have you ever felt like you were in a battle, the blows continue to come? At times it feels like you're in a battlefield, with no weapons. As Christians we have an opponent that wants nothing more than to bring defeat, and blow after blow after blow comes and we look around and it tends to feel like we cannot gather ourselves from the last blow that was thrown. You find yourself reading the bible, going to church, fellowshipping with other believers and blows continue to come, causing you to feel discouraged.

Well I am thankful you chose to pick up *"Are you Suited and Ready for Battle"*, the guide that will not only impact your life, but transform your life. If anyone knows what you're going through in this season of your life it is the Author, Pastor Karen. *"Are you Suited and Ready for Battle"* was written from a deep place within Pastor Karen, a place where loss took place, rejection took place, a place that is familiar with what it takes to reclaim your destiny over your life.

I have known Pastor Karen for 20 years, through these years I have seen how she dealt with the battles that came her way. I have seen how when she lost her husband, she went through a time of solitude with the Lord, how He rekindled her, how He reminded her of her destiny, how He spoke to her and reassured her and through every word He spoke into her life, He was dressing her for the next battle she would go into.

Please note when you read this book, the Author is not speaking from of place that she is not aware of, she is very familiar with the tactics of the enemy and has created this guide to assist every believer through the blows, through the spiritual warfare that they will face on their Christian journey.

I am proud and admire the zeal, and strength within Pastor Karen, as the reader my prayer is that you continue to remain encouraged, and know that you don't fight for victory, you fight *from* Victory. Blessings!

Pastor Veronica Dixon

Founder of "She Blossoms By Being R.E.A.L

INTRODUCTION

First and foremost, I dedicate the ministry of this book to the Love of My Life, my Lord and Savior Jesus Christ. Thank You very much for Your unfailing love and patience in propelling me forward in Your work. You have tirelessly and diligently worked with me. I am forever grateful to You for Loving me, not because of me but rather, in *spite* of me. Thank You for trusting me to get this message out to Your Body – the Body of Christ. Without You, it would not have been possible. If it had been left up to me, things would never have gotten off the ground, but with You *"all things are possible."* This is why I am so glad that You are in control and not me.

Natasha Draper (formerly Washington) and Terrell Washington, my two lovely, blessed children of God. The Lord has a lot in store for you and my prayer is that He will increase your hearing His Voice and my dream is that I have the opportunity to witness the two of you walking in the fullness of His calling on your lives.

Ricky, my grandson (the first one to make me a "Nana"), you have been a joy since the day you arrived on this earth – if I am ever having a "stressful" day all I need to do is picture your beautiful face and think of you, and instantly my day is made better. I love you. Jeremiah John Davis, my second and equally a special grandson, I love you, your big beautiful eyes just light up my life, I cannot wait to see what the Lord has in store for you.

To the two people that the Lord used as vehicles to bring me into this world. I love you Mom (Dorothy Carver) and Dad, the late Arthur Jordan Carver– Knowing that you believed in any and everything that I have set my heart and mind to. Mom, your introduction to the world of reading is forever in my mind – you nurtured me and taught me so much. To this day, I still remember you sharing your favorite short stories with me.

WHAT IS SPIRITUAL WARFARE?

"*Finally my brethren, be strong in the Lord and in the power of his might. Put on the whole armor of God, that you may be able to stand against the wiles of the devil. For we do not wrestle against flesh and blood, but against principalities, against powers, against the rulers of the darkness of this age, against spiritual hosts of wickedness in the heavenly places. Therefore take up the whole armor of God, that you may be able to withstand in the evil day, and having done all, to stand. Stand therefore, having **girded your waist with truth**, having put on the **breastplate of righteousness**, and having **shod your feet with the preparation of the gospel of peace**; above all, taking the **shield of faith** with which you will be able to quench all the fiery darts of the wicked one. And take the **helmet of salvation**, and the **sword of the Spirit**, which is the word of God; **praying always** with all prayer and supplication in the Spirit, being watchful to this end with all perseverance and supplication for all the saints…*"
(Ephesians 6:14-17 NKJV)

Firstly, what is Spiritual Warfare? And who is behind it all? Spiritual warfare is a very real issue; one which we will be fighting until we leave this earth. It is one of the most confusing and misunderstood subjects that we as believers face; an issue that many people have countless questions and even fewer answers about. Secondly, spiritual warfare is waged by an invisible enemy, and his invisibility complicates this fact; he is pure evil, this enemy is the complete embodiment of darkness. It is one thing to engage in battle with someone or something that we can see but a completely different matter when we are attempting to engage in battle with "something" or "someone" whom we cannot see. When this is the case, it is seemingly virtually impossible to successfully engage in war. So now, since this is the case, we need all of the help that we can muster up; our help in fighting this enemy is only going to be possible when we seek help from an expert and that expert is God Almighty. Satan has many tactics he uses against us; the bible has many names for him and the *"accuser of the brethren"* is one of them. He would have us Believers think that we are the worst Christian walking on this earth, and because many Believers are unfamiliar with the Word of God, don't have a personal relationship with Jesus and the things He says about us, causes many to actually fall for and believe the lies of this enemy of ours. Now, the bible says about the believer that *"There is now no condemnation to those who are in Christ Jesus, who do not walk according to the flesh but according to the Spirit..."* (Romans 8:1 NKJV). So now, if I've been a student of the Word, I would know this, however; if a person doesn't know this, then he/she will spend an unnecessary amount of time trying to be 'good enough' or 'do something' in order for God to love him/her; or trying to 'work his/her way into heaven' not realizing that their place in heaven is already secured.

INTRODUCTION

Have you ever wondered 'why'? Why so many Christians are being defeated in their walk with The Lord or why for that matter are you being defeated in your walk with The Lord? I'm glad that you asked, just as I also asked this question for many years. Now, sit back and prepare yourself because this book is designed to help you answer this most pressing question. The things you will read and learn concerning the subject of Spiritual Warfare has validity because the book was specifically birthed out of very real experiences which the author encountered over the years, always with the question of *"Is it only me?"* or *"Isn't there anyone else who experiences this terror?"* While going through these experiences, I had absolutely no idea what in the world was going on and happening to me. I had no idea whatsoever that it had a name, and that name is Spiritual Warfare! Why wasn't I ever told about this? Simply put, it's a subject many are not brave enough to tackle and there are many different reasons for their hesitancy, one of the main ones being the "F" word, "FEAR!" Welcome to a new way of viewing and understanding the subject of Spiritual Warfare; my hope and prayer is that you do not think there is anything spooky or weird while reading this book and while not every Christian is going to experience it in the same way, we all do experience it; we are all without a doubt, the object of Satan's attacks. Spiritual Warfare is as real as the reality of Jesus Christ; Satan does not and never will compare to or be greater than our Lord and Savior Jesus the Christ, Jesus is above all and over all. He said, *"I am the Alpha and the Omega, the Beginning and the End, the First and the Last"* (Revelation 22:13 NKJV) I never had much of a desire to even contemplate learning much about Spiritual Warfare and as long as I was in this state of denial and avoidance, to my detriment, I was defenseless and defeated against Satan's attacks. And likewise you, as a Christian will find yourself in the same state if you adopt the attitude that I once had. Look we need to understand that Satan, because he studies our every move, knows all he needs to know about us in order to successfully carry out his harassment, his planned attacks on us throughout our lifetime. When Jesus was born, Satan attempted to take His life by using Herod the King to kill all of the boys under the age of two. *"The Herod, when he saw that he was deceived by the wise men, was exceedingly angry; and he sent forth and put to death all the male children who were I Bethelem and in all its districts, from two years old and under; according to the time which he had determined from the wise men."* (Matthew 2:16 NKJV). So now, we must understand that if he attempted to take the life of *Jesus*, then he surely doesn't have a problem making attempts on our lives. Satan knows and understands exactly what mode of attack he has in mind to use against us in order to get us sidetracked. He doesn't only come at us in the middle of the night under the cover of darkness he is so bold as to come to bother us in the broad daylight in various ways. He has various tools in his arsenal which he uses against us and unfortunately, instead of becoming prepared and knowledgeable, some believers prefer instead to make the terrible mistake of thinking *"If I don't bother him, he won't bother me"* and this type of thinking is fatalistic to our Christian walk and detrimental to one's spiritual life. Once we commit our lives to the Lord, we have by default, enlisted in the army, God's army! Whether or not we want to be in it; that is exactly where we will ultimately end up, smack dab in the middle of warfare. Just as if we were in the U.S. Army, and have a need to go to Basic Training, we must also go through Basic Training in the Army of the Lord. We cannot allow the enemy to cause us to tremble and fear at the sound of his name; he and his demons should be the ones trembling and fearful at the thought of us becoming armed and dangerous against his attacks, *really* finding out who he is; really becoming armed and dangerous against his tactics. He has an army and a very precise battle plan with which to pull his attacks against us. When a soldier goes to war a battle plan is received from the Commander and we in the army of the Lord also have a Commander and His name is Jesus and He likewise has battle plans for us but we first need to report to duty!

In order to learn more about this army in which we are now enlisted, I will equate it to the U.S. Army and parallel our enlisting in the army of Christ to someone enlisting in the United States Army. Enlisting in the Military is done in two parts; the first part is a trip to what is called Military Entrance Processing Station better known as "MEPS" (which is a Department of Defense joint-service organization); during that trip, an individual's physical qualifications, aptitude, and moral standards are determined. Should all of these comply with military standards, then comes clearance for a second trip to MEPS for final processing for transfer to basic training, and further should the person opt to, a career in the U.S. Army is begun. *(Information gathered from Royzell Washington Retired U.S. Army Sergeant First Class (E7).* Some people make it their lifelong career and spend twenty or more years in the service and then retire. However; there is no retiring from the service of the Lord while we are still living; our retirement will come at our demise or The Lord's return; the way that our career in this army begins is a person confesses with the mouth believing with the heart that God raised Jesus Christ from the dead and that person is saved (Romans 10:9 NKJV) and thus recruitment into God's army has begun. In God's army, there is no such luxury, no such thing as going to "basic training" for six weeks and then being shipped to a duty station, no that's not how this particular service works. This war began as soon as we are adopted into God's family. However, we should not be disheartened because unlike the wars in the natural, this one already has a victorious ending. It was actually fought and won over three thousand years ago on a cross on Calvary and our enemy was made a public spectacle of by Jesus! There is no paperwork to sign, no oath to take, just a believing heart and it is done! This book will explain who we are in Christ; who our enemy is; how the enemy works and with the help of the Holy Spirit how we can be victorious in this walk. Despite the intensity of this battle, we can be steadfast and immovable, always abounding in the work of the Lord, and never forgetting the war has already been won by Jesus!

1

SATAN'S STRATEGIES

Though Satan has many different strategies and ways in which he attempts to harm us we must never lose sight of the fact that God is ultimately still in charge. However; it would behoove us to remember that Satan is the master of deception and there are things which we must guard against in our fight with him. He has many plans and devices with which he wars against the child of God. Satan can do no harm to God; he is defeated and because of his defeat he is mad! He's mad because, at one point in time, he had it all, then because of his pride, he got kicked out of heaven! *"...you were the seal of perfection, full of wisdom and perfect in beauty. You were in Eden, the garden of God; every precious stone was your covering: the Sardius, topaz, and diamond, beryl, onyx, and jasper, sapphire, turquoise, and emerald with gold. The workmanship of your timbrels and pipes was prepared for you on the day you were created. You were the anointed cherub who covers; I established you; you were on the holy mountain of God;*

you walked back and forth in the midst of fiery stones. You were perfect in your ways from the day you were created, till iniquity was found in you" (Ezekiel 28:12-15 NKJV). *"... Your heart was lifted up because of your beauty; you corrupted your wisdom for the sake of your splendor; I cast you to the ground..."* (Ezekiel 28:17 NKJV). Yes, at one time he was the beautiful Lucifer, the 'angel' of all angels, worship leader in heaven, but then he begins to believe he could become greater than God, took steps to do so, and was promptly cast out of heaven. *"How you have fallen from heaven, O morning star, son of the morning! How you are cast down to the ground, you who have weakened the nations! For you have said in your heart: 'I will ascend into heave, I will exalt my throne above the stars of God; I will also sit on the mount of the congregation on the farthest sides of the north; I will ascend above the heights of the clouds, I will be like the Most High. Yet you shall be brought down to Sheol to the lowest depths of the Pit"* (Isaiah 14:12-15 NKJV). He is livid because he can *never* again obtain that position and because he can do no harm to God, he attacks the *children* of God. Satan hates the Believer with a vengeance! He is very precise and strategic in his attacks; he has a plethora of arsenal and devices at his disposal (his fiery darts). I can just imagine him in the dark outer places with his demons surrounding him poised and ready to follow his every command as they are dispersed to do evil on the earth; there are platoons upon platoons of fallen angels, ready to do his bidding, These willing vessels upon which he depends are the 1/3 of heavens angels who rebelled with him and likewise were cast down from heaven. Just as the Commander barks out orders to his platoons, *"prepare to go to battle, prepare to attack, this is what our manner of attack today will be..."* on and on it goes I'm sure is the same scene with Satan and his demons. Nevertheless, we as children of the Most High God have the help of heaven at our disposal, all the help we will ever need is available; we have the very power of God on the inside of us, the Holy Spirit. As well as our angel, which God has given us; His holy angels to assist us in our daily walk. *"To which of the angels did God ever say, 'Sit at my right hand til I make your enemies your footstool' Are they not all ministering spirits set forth to minister for those who will inherit salvation?* (Hebrews 1:13-14 NKJV). From the beginning of time, satan has attempted to thwart the work of God in the lives of the children of God; one example of this type of attack is when he attempted to stop the angel who was sent in response to Daniel's prayer. *"...Do not fear, Daniel, for from the first day that you set your heart to understand, and to humble yourself before God, your words were heard; and I have come because of your words. But the prince of the kingdom of Persia withstood me twenty-one days; and behold, Michael, one of the chief princes, came to help me..."* (Daniel 10:12-13 NKJV). Likewise, early on in the life of the believer, Satan begins to prepare his activities and evil plans in order to attempt to cause the Believer to detour or even stop the person from coming to know God through Jesus. Satan causes all sorts of pain in the person's life so that hopefully the person will not become a believer, a child of God. One of the first of many strategies he used is death. As stated earlier, his first attempt at killing was when Jesus was born, Satan used Herod the king to accomplish his task of having all boys two years old and under killed with the hopes that Jesus would be in the number. *"...was exceedingly angry; and he sent forth and put to death all the male children who were in Bethlehem and in all its districts, from two years old and under…"* (Matthew 2:16 NKJV). But God had an escape route in place. He saved Jesus from the plans of the enemy and the same way that He made an escape route for Joseph the earthly father of Jesus to escape and save Jesus and Mary from the hands of Herod, He has done the same for the Believer, God thwarts the plans of the enemy. However, it's still to be expected that Satan will continue to harass the believer until either death or the return of Jesus.

His causing the believer to doubt d Adam could be disobedient to God without consequence. In his dialogue with Eve, he was able to convince her that she and Adam had a right to disobey God, all this without her even being aware that she in his clutches, was being deceived. "Now the serpent was more cunning than any beast of the field which the Lord God had made. And he said to the woman, 'Has God indeed said, 'You shall not eat of every tree of the garden'? And the woman said to the serpent, 'ay eat the fruit of the trees of the garden: but of the fruit of the tree which is in the midst of the garden, God has said, 'You shall not eat it, nor sha*ll*

This is not some fictitious story. This is real. I never really understood why I had to endure the many Spiritual attacks that I did, I never fully understood what I was dealing with what was really happening, and certainly did not know how to respond. Until one night in 2004, I was enduring yet another attack. As I became awake, I began to cry and say to the Lord *"Lord, why does this keep happening to me"* and *"where are my angels that you promised would protect me, why aren't you helping me?"* Then I became silent and just lay there crying and almost without me noticing, the Spirit of the Lord began to say over and over in my Spirit *'submit to God, resist the devil and he'll flee'* as well as *'greater is He that is in you than he that is in the world.'* Over and over I heard these words until I finally began to open my mouth and speak them aloud, and instantly I began to notice a peace beginning to flood my spirit and I began to thank and worship God. After I became calm again, the Lord began to speak to me and His words were *'You had to go through that, if you had not YUexperienced that then how would you be able to tell others that this is real but that I can deliver them?'* I have an obligation to tell it because as long as God's people are unaware and unprepared, we are defeated and unable to overcome the enemy just as it happened that lonely night as I lay in my bed alone in a hotel room thousands of miles from home in late 2004. It wasn't that God was not there, simply put, I didn't "believe" that He was there. I *thought* I believed He was there but I later realized that in fact, I had not.

It's time that the Church wake up! It is time that we begin to take God at His Word, Jesus said that "if" we believe, we would do greater things than He did. He healed many as well as cast out demons and commanded them to *"return no more,"* and we should be doing the same, and if we would only look around us we will see that seemingly we are not really believing, it is not happening! And the only reason it is not happening is because of Unbelief! I believe Christ is weeping over His church. Weeping because we are living far below our potential, not living the abundant life that He died to give us. He said if we can *"only believe!"* Yes, it's true, we are in a battle but it's a battle that was won thousands of years ago *"...Death has been swallowed up in victory. O Death, where is your sting? O Hades, where is your victory?..."* (1 Corinthians

15:55 NKJV). Jesus told His disciples *"...These things I have spoken to you, that in Me you may have peace. In the world you will have tribulation; but be of good cheer; I have overcome the world..."* (John 16:33 NKJV). Though it did not appear to be, Jesus had the victory when He went to the cross, died, bled and rose from the grave.

Paul has given us the 'secret' to waging war against the enemy, everything we need to fight is found in the armor – notice Paul said *"full armor of God."* Paul explains the full armor of God best in Ephesians 6:10-17. To have on the armor without the knowledge of how to use it can be likened to being in a full-blown war with a fully loaded machine gun just standing around, holding it in your hands not knowing how to use it; this spells sure defeat! So now, this is the state I found myself in and instead of things getting better, things continued to get worse and worse as Satan continued to harass me, I began to experience more and more spiritual attacks against my body and I was in terrible fear, afraid to be alone in the house with the lights out, afraid to be alone period and in all of this, I never realized that the Lord had a purpose for it all. The Lord was working where I could not recognize it and He was teaching me without me even being aware of the lesson. I suffered in silence because I was so sure that no one would believe me. I believe the Lord allowed the attacks to become more and more intense so that eventually I would have to face and deal with them. I endured them for approximately five years before I decided that *"enough is enough!"* I like to compare it to being bullied in school for years and years before finally standing up to the bully only to realize that he, underneath all of the harassment, was really afraid of me! This is how it is with the devil, our enemy, he is actually afraid and intimidated by the child of God, therefore his battle plan is to try to get us to fear him before we understand and begin to walk in the power that we have in God and cast him out with just one word (Jesus). Sad to say, that's exactly the position he had me in, one of intense fear; until finally, I experienced the worst attack of my life. I didn't know what to do so I was always ending up spiritually bruised and afraid. As what typically happens in our lives, facing certain circumstances forces us to make real, hard choices; the following explanation of the intense, life-changing encounter was an experience with spiritual warfare which pushed me to make the choice of getting serious and educating others concerning this subject or turning and running away as I had done for so many years previously. I understood that this is where I had to make a choice! I could either sink or swim. I made the conscious decision to swim and now, I have the awesome opportunity *and* responsibility of passing on this invaluable information to my brothers and sisters in the Lord.

2

PERSONAL ENCOUNTER WITH SPIRITUAL WARFARE

As I lay in my bed in a state of semiconsciousness, drifting off to sleep, I could sense in the spirit that something was about to happen. As I attempted to come fully awake, I found myself totally paralyzed. A demon spirit was literally holding me down on the bed and because my strength was no match for his, I could do nothing. This evil, the vile thing had an iron grip on me. *(Remember now this was all an encounter in the Spirit).* And because I could not use my mouth I immediately began to 'say' *"Jesus, Jesus"* in my mind; however, in spite of the fact that I was "saying" *'Jesus, Jesus,'* nothing was happening; (not because Jesus was not able, but because my faith was not yet active. Though I was "saying" *'Jesus,'* there was still fear in my heart). Next, I began to pray for God to send my protecting angels. Immediately, the Spirit of God prompted my Spirit with the words '*I worship God in heaven,*' and instantly in my mind I began to repeat '*I worship God in Heaven.*' I continued doing so over and over while the demon attempted to stop my confession by covering my mouth. All that I recall of this awful experience is feeling what seemed to be a long clawlike, cold and wet nail and a hairy finger laying across the lower part of my face onto my lip. As I was in the midst of this battle, and repeating '*Jesus, Jesus,*' initially because of the fear, there really was no belief in my heart, nothing which showed that I *knew without a doubt that* He was there and because this fear was overtaking me, my faith was essentially nonexistent. However; as I continued to worship God with my confession of '*I worship God in Heaven,*' right there in the midst of it all, I began to finally 'believe' my confession and knew without a shadow of a doubt to whom my worship was going; thus the devil then had no choice but to flee. I liken this to the account of Jehoshaphat who, in the midst of battle, instead of becoming afraid, he "*…appointed those who should sing to the Lord, and who should praise the beauty of holiness, as they went out before the army and were saying 'praise the Lord for His mercy endures forever.…*" (2 Chronicles 20:21 NKJV). Now, as I stated earlier, this was a hideous, evil experience. I don't know that this was necessarily a physical attack but as Paul said in scripture "*…I know a man who fourteen years ago was caught up to the third heaven whether it was in the body or not I do not know…*" (2 Corinthians 12:2); I now say "*I know a woman who was caught in a battle, whether it was in the body or not, I do not know.*" This is how it was with me that fateful night…

Oh people of God! There is a fierce, fierce battle raging around us, but we must take heart because this battle is not ours, it is truly the Lord's (2 Chronicles 20:15). The Word of God will never be real in our lives as long as we only read it and never apply it. *"But be doers of the Word, and not hearers only, deceiving yourselves. For if anyone is a hearer of the Word and not a doer, he is like a man observing his natural face in a mirror; for he observes himself, goes away, and immediately forgets what kind of man he was..."* (James 1:22-24 NKJV). Without faith, the Word will never be active and real in any of our lives. As Jesus told the woman with the issue of blood *"...your faith has made you well..."* (Matthew 9:22 NKJV). James said *"...Thus also faith by itself, if it does not have works is dead..."* (James 2:17 NKJV). Likewise, scripture tells us that without it (faith), it is impossible to please God; *"By faith Enoch was taken away so that he did not see death, and was not found, because God had taken him... for before he was taken he had this testimony, that he pleased God. But without faith it is impossible to please Him, for he who comes to God must believe that He is, and that He is a rewarder of those who diligently seek Him...* (Hebrews 11:5-6 NKJV). Now, the question becomes "how do I practice this faith in my life?" The answer to that is a simple one. Though we don't typically like to endure trials, we can rejoice and not forget that faith is produced in *the midst of them.*

Likewise, worship is a mode of praise unto the Lord...

The men began to sing praises to the Lord, and He gave them the victory. *"...Now when they began to sing and to praise, the Lord set ambushes against the people of Ammon, Moab, and Mount Seir, who had come against Judah; and they were defeated...* (2 Chronicles 20:22 NKJV). There is also another account in scripture of the seven sons of Sceva who very foolishly attempted to cast out a demon in the same way they had witnessed *Paul* do it; however, since they lacked the authority *and* the confidence in God which Paul had, they found that they themselves because they had no relationship with Jesus Christ, and did not serve Him nor did they acknowledge Him, were defeated and made a spectacle of. *"…then some of the itinerant Jewish exorcists took it upon themselves to call the name of the Lord Jesus over those who had evil spirits, saying 'We exorcise you by the Jesus whom Paul preaches. Also there were seven sons of Sceva, a Jewish chief priest, who did so. And the evil spirit answered and said, 'Jesus I know, and Paul I know; but who are you?' Then the man in whom the evil spirit was leaped on them, overpowered them, and prevailed against them, so that they fled out of that house naked and wounded…"* (Acts 19:13-16 NKJV). The unprepared believer will attempt to fight this battle in the flesh; to logically figure it out, not realizing that the weapons of our warfare are not carnal but spiritual; therefore, it must be fought in a totally different way, it must be approached through prayer which is not the norm.

DIFFERENT PIECES OF THE ARMOR

"Finally be strong in the Lord and in his mighty power. Put on the full armor of God so that you can take your stand against the devil's schemes. For our struggle is not against flesh and blood, but against the rulers, against the authorities, against the powers of this dark world and against the spiritual forces of evil in the heavenly realms. Therefore put on the full armor of God, so that when the day of evil comes, you may be able to stand your ground, and after you have done everything, to stand. Stand firm then, with the belt of truth buckled around your waist, with the breastplate of righteousness in place, and with your feet fitted with the readiness that comes from the

gospel of peace. In addition to all of this, take up the shield of faith, with which you can extinguish all the flaming arrows of the evil one. Take the helmet of salvation and the sword of the Spirit, which is the word of God. And pray in the Spirit on all occasions with all kinds of prayers and requests..." (Ephesians 6:10 – 18 NLT). As Paul admonishes us to put on the whole armor, he sums it up before continuing on to name the individual pieces of armor.

In the early days of my walk with the Lord, I would oftentimes pose the question to Him *"What exactly does it mean to put on the whole armor of God?"* As I spent much time in prayer waiting for the answer, this is what the Lord impressed in my spirit, and in the remainder of this book I will set about explaining the process so that you too can with confidence answer the question posed in the title of this book; *"Yes, I am Suited and Ready for Battle"* The way that we put on the whole armor of God is to familiarize ourselves with His word by reading, studying, obeying His word on a daily basis. When Jesus was being tempted in the desert by Satan the battle was not fought in "the flesh," He spoke the Word of God, by beginning each response with *"It is written..."* (this account can be found in Matthew 4). So now further, we also must continually go before Him in prayer. *"Therefore put on the whole armor of God that you may be able to stand against wiles of the devil."* In order to be able to stand whenever we are attacked by the enemy, we must cover ourselves with the whole armor of God.

When Jesus was preparing to leave His disciples and go to the cross. He told them that the Holy Spirit would bring all things to their remembrance; now the way that God speaks to us His children is by our Spirit and through His Word and if we don't fill our Spirits with His Word, then the Holy Spirit has nothing to "bring back" to our remembrance. However; if we are diligent in studying His Word, then we too can say like King David said *"...Your Word I have hidden in my heart that I might not sin against You..."* (Psalm 119:11 NKJV).

Let's look at the various parts of the armor and see how they help us. Paul tells us we need it so that we can stand against the schemes of the enemy. *"...Therefore take up the whole armor of God, that you may be able to withstand in the evil day, and having done all, to stand"* (Ephesians 6:13 NKJV).

3

PURPOSE OF INDIVIDUAL PIECES OF THE ARMOR

Loins (waist) girt about with the belt of **Truth**

Breastplate of **Righteousness**

Feet shod with the preparation of the **Gospel of Peace**

Shield of **Faith**

Helmet of **Salvation**

Sword of the Spirit (Word of God)

Praying always

"The Belt of Truth - Psalm 51:6"

Truth is the absence of deceit; God is truth, He is the embodiment and the essence of *Truth*, therefore He desires for it to permeate every fiber of our being. *"Behold, You desire truth in the inward parts..."* (Psalm 51:6 NKJV), He (Jesus) said, *"...I am the Way, the Truth, and the life..."* (John 14:6 NKJV). Now then, if our loins, our waist; the center of our physical body, the very core, the essence of who we are is permeated with *Truth*, then we will always find ourselves walking fully in it, at every opportunity; the essence of God in us is birthed and will never cease to bring forth life; the very life, the essence of Jesus Christ! The belt of truth involves two places; our hearts and our minds. Truth keeps us secure in Christ and makes all the other pieces of armor effective. The belt of truth holds our armor in place. Paul said it best *"...for in Him we live and move and have our being..."* (Acts 17:28). Commit yourself daily to walk in the light of God's truth. *"Teach me your way, O Lord; I will walk in Your truth..."* (Psalm 86:11 NKJV). This explains why the enemy attempts to stop the process of us growing in God everyday of our lives; he will even attempt to keep us bound by some secret sin or shame so that we will not be found to be walking in complete truth with God. Satan does not want us to be secure in who Jesus is in and through us; and the way he (satan) achieves this is by attempting to get us to be out of fellowship (a break in intimacy and communion) with God by way of unconfessed sin in our lives; living a lie, always under a cloud of self-condemnation. Just the mere fact that *Truth* brings forth life is repulsive to him because all he knows how to do is operate in deceit, darkness, and lies. That is his modus operandi (m.o.). He is a liar and the father of lies. ...*You are of your father the devil, and the desires of your father you want to do. He was a murderer from the beginning, and does not stand in the truth, because there is no truth in him. When he speaks a lie, he speaks from his own resources, for he is a liar and the father of it...*" (John 8:44 NKJV). When we begin to hold onto and understand the truth, the enemy never has anything with which to hold us in bondage. The truth makes us free. "*...and you will know the truth, and the truth will make you free...*" (John 8:32 NKJV). We will be free from shame, hurt, embarrassment, condemnation, etc... anything that keeps us in the trap of ungodliness. Truth is light and it exposes the darkness and by having it buckled around the very core of our lives it becomes a powerful weapon against the enemy. In addition to this, if we know the truth and have it in our inner parts, which is knowing Jesus and obeying His word, this likewise proves to be a powerful weapon which we use to fight against the fiery darts of the enemy. We are set free from his bondage. Satan will continually attempt to drag us back down with the bondage which makes us *think* we are under *his* control. Just as he was tempting Jesus in the wilderness; after Jesus commanded him to go away and return no more, the bible says that "*...he* (satan) *departed for a more opportune time...*" so it is with us. When we are set free from him, he waits for a more opportune time to come back and try to catch us with our guard down and put us in bondage, much worse than we were in the beginning. "*When an unclean spirit goes out of a man, he goes through dry places, seeking rest; and finding none, he says, 'I will return to my house from which I came.' And when he comes, he finds it swept and put in order. Then he goes and takes with him seven* *other spirits more wicked than himself, and they enter and dwell there; and the last state of that man is worse than the first..."* (Luke 11:24-26 NKJV). This is why it is imperative that we fill ourselves with God's Word; so that when the enemy does return he will not find a house swept clean and **empty** that he can overtake with his seven friends. He wants us to believe that we are and will always be under his control, but that could not be farther from the truth and, if we are not familiar with the Word of God, we will never be effectively equipped in this battle. Once we come into the glorious knowledge of God's Word, we then begin to walk in it, stand firm and take a "defensive" as well an "offensive" stand against this enemy of ours. Notice in verse 26, the scripture says that the evil spirit and his friends *"enter and dwell there;"* how presumptuous of him! He has the audacity to attempt to come into *our* house and *dwell* there. He acts as if he has the *right* to be there! This very fact makes me indignant and should cause the same reaction in you. We are blood-bought children of the Most High God and the enemy of our souls has the nerve to attempt to come and barge into our home (spirit) and settle there as if he has the right! This is why we as Believer's need to be familiar with the Word of God, know Who He is and who we are from His (God's) perspective; we would know and understand that we have absolutely no dealings with darkness and he (the devil) has to flee. We would truly know and understand this glorious truth and the truth, as the bible says, *"will make us free"* from all deception of the devil. How is this glorious truth achieved? The way *Truth* is achieved is through our personal relationship with Jesus. If our relationship with Jesus is not a top priority, first in our lives, once again we will be doing things in our own strength (trying to figure it out without seeking God but rather seeking to fix it through other means) and then eventually end up in danger of once again walking with the enemy of our soul. However, when we are in a personal relationship with Jesus, we can know and hold tightly to the truth of God. No longer will the lies of the enemy be our "truth".... When we are under the influence, or rather in a relationship with the enemy, we will only hear and believe his lies. It is so very important that we do not take for granted our relationship with Jesus; very important that we at all times gauge where we are in our standing with Him at any given time. In our earthly relationships, we must always be careful to not take them for granted, ever mindful of maintaining intimacy; it is the same with our relationship with Jesus; even more so. There are many, many outside influences vying for our attention and if we are not careful we will succumb and ultimately end up in a lukewarm, barely there, relationship with Jesus. God desires a red-hot, intense, intimate relationship with Him through Jesus the Christ (Anointed One). If our relationship with Him is lukewarm at best, halfheartedly trudging along, never victorious, always succumbing to the attacks and temptations of the devil then we will find ourselves backsliding. However, when we are in a vibrant, exciting daily fellowship with God, we cannot, and will not go wrong, This is not to say that we won't stumble and fall at times but *when* we do, we will do like David did and immediately have a heart of repentance, turning away from the sin that has ensnared us and get back in right relationship with God. I mean since we have to be in this world with its deceitfulness, pain, confusion, etc… wouldn't it make more sense to remain close to our heavenly Father? Now it very important to understand that this relationship building will take some time to develop, but it is time well spent and definitely worth the effort.

It does not happen automatically, it only comes over time and as we see His faithfulness and care for us; we understand that it is imperative that we spend time with Him – quality time, not just five minutes as we leave out of the house in the morning with a *"Lord, watch over me"* prayer. Though that can be a starting point, we must spend quality time with Him throughout the day. We can do that anywhere; constantly communing with Him, always with our mind stayed on Him. God *"You will keep him in perfect peace, whose mind is stayed on You..."* (Isaiah 26:3 NKJV). That is a step toward further building our trust in Him – when we eventually find ourselves in a storm but having an indescribable amount of calmness and peace. *"Be anxious for nothing, but in everything by prayer and supplication, with thanksgiving, let your requests be made known to God; and the peace of God, which surpasses all understanding will guard your hearts and minds through Christ Jesus..."* (Philippians 4:6-7 NKJV). We begin to experience His care for us. When others come against us, we will see God's provision, we will see the Lord redeem "His servants." We will not be condemned when we take refuge in Him. *"The Lord redeems the soul of His servants..."* (Psalm 34:22 NKJV). The scripture tells us that if we dwell in His secret place, we will abide in His shadow, then and only then will we have all of the protection we will ever need. And the awesome thing about this is the fact that we need to only abide in His shadow *"...he that dwelleth in the secret place of the Most High, shall abide under the shadow of the Almighty, surely He will save you from the fowlers snare and from the deadly pestilence. He will cover you with His feathers and under*

His wings you will find refuge; his faithfulness will be your shield and rampart..." (Psalm 91:1-4 NKJV). The way we take Him at His Word in order to see the truth in it is, first of all, to dwell which means to remain or reside; in other words "camp out" at His feet. So we must ask "Am I remaining or residing" in Him? Is my prayer life strong in order to stay near Him?" If the answer is in the affirmative and I seemingly don't see His protection, maybe it is because His protection is not what I thought it would or should look like. *"...For My thoughts are not your thoughts, Nor are your ways My ways, says the Lord. For as the heavens are higher than the earth, so are My ways higher than your ways, and My thoughts than your thoughts..."* (Isaiah 55:8-9 NKJV). Something else which may be considered, perhaps we may be in some sort of unconscious way looking for it one way; perhaps the way "I" would do it instead of totally trusting that He is doing it the way He wants to. His Word says *"Trust in the Lord with all your heart and lean not on your own understanding; in all your ways acknowledge Him, and He shall direct your paths. Do not be wise in your own eyes..."* (Proverbs 3:5-7a NKJV). That is what having total trust in our Redeemer means! Trusting him, acknowledging Him and He will make our paths straight! That's a promise! It is as easy as saying *"O.K. God my life is yours"* and having the peace that He's watching over us. Remember He told Jeremiah that he's watching over *his word* to perform it? *"Moreover the word of the Lord came to me saying 'Jeremiah, what do you see?' "And I said 'I see a branch of an almond tree.' "Then the Lord said to me 'You have seen well, for I will hasten My Word to perform it..."* (Jeremiah 1:11-12 NKJV); (one version reads "to fulfill it"). If His word is living and active inside of me then that means He's watching over me, covering me! Praise the Lord! What an awesome revelation! Imagine having this type of truth girded about my loins. My waist, the center of my being where life resides. Jesus did say *"I am the way, the truth and the life"* (John 14:6 NKJV). This is precisely what would explain the reason that I, when faced with the greatest spiritual attack of my life didn't *see* a response, when I uttered the words *'Jesus, Jesus'* (I didn't immediately have the "truth" in my inner parts) – I had the knowledge but hallelujah When I began to say with confidence *"I worship God in Heaven,"* the demon had to leave; the *truth* of what I believed activated my faith within me. My faith began to rise up, just like the woman with the blood issue, her belief that by touching the hem of Jesus' garment, healing would flow through her body *"...When she heard about Jesus, she came behind Him in the crowd and touched His garment. For she said, 'If only I may touch His clothes, I shall be made well..."* (Mark 5:27-28 NKJV). Because she had a personal encounter with Him, she *knew*; and Jesus did not disappoint; *"Daughter, your faith has made you well. Go in peace, and be healed of your affliction..."* (Mark 5:34 NKJV). She had faith to believe that the truth of the matter was that this man Jesus had what she needed. Likewise, Job after all of his calamities, was able to eventually say to God *"...I have heard of You by the hearing of the ear, but now my eye sees You. Therefore I abhor myself and repent in dust and ashes."* (Job 42:5-6 NKJV). In other words, he was saying "I had a 'head' knowledge of you but now after all that I've been through, all the pain that I suffered, I have yet experienced an encounter with You; I've had the opportunity to experience Your sovereignty. So it is with us saints, the things that we face, the calamities of living in this sin-filled world causes us to have faith that God is indeed in control as He supernaturally steps into our situations with us. Yes, this is how we understand and apply the *Truth* of God's Word.

"Breastplate of Righteousness"

"To know and walk in the ways of God"

Once again, it must be understood that I'm specifically referring to the Believer in this book and one huge problem I've encountered with a lot of believers is that though many say otherwise, they really do not want the whole truth all of the time; and possibly not really want to *walk* in it. It requires a lot of work on our part in order to really have truth in our inward parts. Because in order to walk in this truth that God desires, we must on a continual basis be in close communion with God. I'm not sure why but perhaps because at times, in reality, the truth can be rather hurtful and sting. Whatever be the reason, many people in the body of Christ actually operate on the outskirts of truth, I mean after all who really wants to hear the truth when it is not favorable to them? When it proves them to be less than honorable at times in their dealings with other people; when it shows them to be not as pure and honest as many may have believed at one time? Very few people will say and actually *mean* that they want the truth, the whole truth, and nothing but the truth. A lot of people have actually convinced themselves that they are honest, truthful, God-fearing individuals when *that* confession in itself is less than honest. And the actual truth is that "truth" is lacking in their conduct as well as speech. "Truth" is one of the things that, either you have it or you don't. We read the story of King David who was faced with his own deceptive heart after he had Bathsheba (another man's wife) brought to him in order to "know her" (have sex with her). *"It happened in the spring of the year, at the time when kings go out to battle, that David sent Joab and his* servants with him, and all Israel; and they destroyed the people of Ammon and besieged Rabbah. But David remained at Jerusalem. Then it happened one evening that David arose from his bed and walked on the roof of the king's house. And from the roof he saw a woman bathing, and the woman was very beautiful to behold. So David sent and inquired about the woman. And someone said, 'Is this not Bathsheba, the daughter of Eliam, the wife of Uriah the Hittite?' Then David sent messengers, and took her, and she came to him and he lay with her, for she was cleansed from her impurity; and she returned to her house. And the woman conceived; so she sent and told David, and said, 'I am with child.' Then David sent to Joab, saying, 'Send me Uriah the Hittite.' And Joab sent Uriah to David. When Uriah had come to him, David asked how Joab was doing, and how the people were doing, and how the war prospered. And David said to Uriah, 'Go down to your house and wash your feet.' So Uriah departed from the king's house, and a gift of food from the king followed him. But Uriah slept at the door of the king's house with all the servants of his lord, and did not go down to his house. So when they told David, saying, 'Uriah did not go down to his house,' David said to Uriah, ' Did you not come from a journey? Why did you not go down to your house?" And Uriah said to David, 'The ark and Israel and Judah are dwelling in tents, and my lord Joab and the servants of my lord are encamped in the open fields. Shall I then go to my house to eat and the servants of my lord are encamped in the open fields. Shall I then go to my house to eat and drink, and lie with my wife? As you live, and as your soul loves, I will not do this thing. Then David said to Uriah, 'Wait here today also, and tomorrow I will let you depart." So Uriah remained in Jerusalem that day and the next. Now when David called him, he ate and drank before him; and he *made him drunk. And at evening he went out to lie on his bed with the servants of his lord, but he did not go down to his house. In the morning, it happened that David wrote a letter to Joab and sent it by the hand of Uriah. And he wrote in the letter, saying, 'Set Uriah in the forefront of the hottest battle, and retreat from him, that he may be struck down and die.' So it was, while Joab besieged the city, that he assigned Uriah to a place where he knew there were valiant men. Then the men of the city came out and fought with Joab. And some of the people of the servants of David fell; and Uriah the Hittite died also"* (2 Samuel 11:1-17 NKJV). Now here we have King David, a man of valor, a man who was handpicked by God to lead the people of God; A man who against all odds was God's chosen one; what could have gone wrong? One day while watching what my husband calls a "who done it" show, a detective who was being interviewed concerning a murder case made a very simple but profound statement. He said, *"Evidence doesn't lie, but people do."* Now we know that all evil is precipitated by Satan himself, Jesus called him the "father of lies." *"…You are of your father the devil, and the desires of your father you want to do. He was a murderer from the beginning, and does not stand in the truth, beause there is no truth in him. When he speaks a lie, he speaks from his own resources, for he is a liar and the father of it"* (John 8:44 NKJV). After this despicable act, he went even further, and in order to cover up his sinful acts and being found to have impregnated another man's wife, he attempted to get her husband drunk and convince him to sleep with her so that it would appear that she was pregnant by her own husband. What he was not counting on was that Bathsheba's husband would be a man of integrity. He refused to take David up on his offer of a night of drinking and pleasure with his own wife while his own fighting men would be left on the battlefield that night; he felt that it was only right that if they had to be in battle, then he too would be in battle right alongside them. Therefore, he respectfully declined David's offer. In light of this new 'problem,' David felt the need to still attempt to 'fix' it, so still trying to "save face" he instead went a much more sinister route. He instead instructed the other fighting men to pretend they were all going to the battle line and when they had Bathsheba's husband there alongside them, they were to all pull back leaving him vulnerable, alone, and ultimately killed.

If we are truthful and honest in our behavior at all times, alone or not, then when no one is watching or a witness to it, the truth will always be evident in our lives. Unfortunately, A lot of people mistakenly believe that they can be honest and truthful some of the time, being less than truthful when it suits their particular situation and then things will be fine; however; nothing can be further from the truth. God is a God of one hundred percent honesty, there are no cutting corners with Him, either come with the whole truth of the counsel of God or don't come at all. He's holy and pure, He is truth, He is the very essence of truth. $99^{1/2}$ will not do!!!

Now the devil, on the other hand, is a liar, as a matter of fact, he is the father of lies; the very essence of deceit. His native language is "lie." As I heard a 'quote' from someone at one time before, *"A lie doesn't care who tells it."* In other words, the devil doesn't care who he gets to actually tell his lies, as long as *someone* does it, then he is satisfied. One thing worth noting here is that we came into the world with an uncanny ability to do wrong, notice that a child never has to be taught to lie or do something dishonest, it comes naturally; a child who is caught doing something wrong never has to be taught to shift the blame or deny any involvement at all. Anyone who has ever caught a child literally with a hand in the cookie jar or actually been the one caught with a hand in the cookie jar knows that the first instinct is to deny any wrongdoing at all and attempt to shift the blame. I remember as a child of approximately ten years of age being caught sneaking candy out of a box on top of the refrigerator, I denied any involvement whatsoever, as a matter of fact, I accused and shifted the blame to my two-year-old cousin as the culprit. The reason that it is so easy to conjure up a lie instantaneously is because of the sinful nature that we were born with. We see it in scripture when Adam and Eve were confronted by God concerning their sin of disobedience when they ate of the fruit, they instantly blamed the "other;" when asked about the part that he played, Adam actually attempted to shift the blame to *God* in a roundabout way *"...the woman whom You gave to be with me, she gave me of the tree, and I ate..."* (Genesis 3:12 NKJV). Then Eve likewise placed the blame elsewhere *"...the serpent deceived me and I ate..."* (Genesis 3:13 NKJV). Not once did either one of them simply say *"Lord, I'm sorry, I messed up, I sinned, I did what you told me not to do..."* The latter response would have gone a whole lot further with God than did their excuses. God loves righteousness; *"You love righteousness and hate wickedness..."* (Psalm 45:7 NKJV). Paul tells us to put on the "breastplate of righteousness" and in order to understand this; we will look at it from the viewpoint of an armored soldier. When an armored soldier was outfitted with the breastplate, it literally covered the front part of his body down to the waist and was made of iron or iron-like material; a very durable material that was impossible to penetrate. This allowed the soldier to have total confidence that if by chance, any ammunition from his enemy was to strike it, he himself would be protected from harm. Likewise, when a person has put on the "Breastplate of Righteousness" there is always a new swagger if you will, the person can then begin to walk with a newfound confidence even when the devil is constantly attacking with lies and accusations and constantly reminding them of their past sins. Without the Breastplate of Righteousness, these fiery darts will penetrate the heart and spell sure defeat for the child of God; it is imperative that we know who we are in Jesus so that we can approach the throne of God the way He intended us to do, boldly. *"Let us then approach the throne of grace with confidence, so that we may receive mercy and find grace to help us in our time of need"* (Hebrews 4:16 NKJV).

As stated above, the breastplate was an object that covered the whole chest area and anyone who knows anything about the anatomy knows that, of course, our heart is in our chest, if we don't have a heart then there is no life. Of course, there are other vital organs which "reside" in the chest cavity but let's look at it from the heart's standpoint. If righteousness is part of the armor that will also sustain us in this battle, it stands to reason that it is very important in the life of the believer. Scripture tells us that all of the righteous are rewarded, *"…the Lord rewards every man for his righteousness, and faithfulness…"* (1 Samuel 26:23 NKJV).

Righteousness is defined as *"uprightness, justice, blamelessness.* Christ's righteousness is credited to our account and makes us holy before God. *"acting in accord with divine or moral law; free from guilt or sin..."* Once we know and begin to walk in the way of righteousness, we *will* be rewarded, now that's not to say we won't face trials in this world because we will, *"...you will have tribulation; but be of good cheer, I have overcome the world..."* (John 16:33 NKJV). However God rewards us *"...and that he rewards those who diligently seek him."* (Hebrews 11:6 NKJV). We see a great illustration of someone who is diligently seeking the Lord and His righteousness, King David was this man. Though far from perfect, he was always striving to be righteous in God's eyesight; he was even at one point by God, referred to as *"A Man after My own heart."* After taking the kingdom away from the hands of Saul, God appointed David *"You acted foolishly,"* Samuel said. *"You have not kept the command the Lord your God gave you; if you had, he would have established your kingdom over Israel for all time. But now your kingdom will not endure; the Lord has sought out a man after his own heart and appointed him leader of his people* (David's reward)*, because you* (Saul) *have not kept the Lord's command."* (1 Samuel 13:13-14 NKJV).

When we read further on in 1 Samuel, we see that Saul was very angry and jealous, even attempting to kill David several times; many times David was forced to literally run for his life. When reading scripture, we get many opportunities to see the state of David's heart concerning Saul; though he had many different "perfect" opportunities to kill the one who was trying to harm him, David exemplified the character of a true man of God and refused to bring any harm to Saul. *"The Lord rewards every man for his righteousness and faithfulness. The Lord delivered you into my hands today, but I would not lay a hand on the Lords anointed..."*

(1 Samuel 26:23 NKJV). David knew that God would not approve of him retaliating against Saul by laying a hand on him, *"...who can lay a hand on the Lord's anointed and be guiltless..."* (2 Samuel 26:9 NKJV). David was walking in righteousness, he was walking in uprightness; though many others would have taken advantage of that opportunity to get revenge, David refused. He, *"a man after Gods own heart"* did what was right in the sight of God; he knew that God would handle Saul in His time *"...the Lord himself will strike him, either his time will come and he will die, or he will go into battle and die..."* (1 Samuel 26:10 NKJV). In other words, David refused to interfere in God's business; David was doing what Jesus admonished us to do when He said: *"...but seek first His kingdom and His righteousness..."* (Matthew 6:33 NKJV). We are to actually seek out His righteousness, go looking for it; always looking for opportunities to live righteously. Scripture tells us that *"Abraham believed God, and it was credited to him as righteousness"* (Romans 4:3 NKJV). Paul also says *"...God credits righteousness apart from works"* (Romans 4:6 NKJV). God credited righteousness apart from works because one has nothing to do with the other. Righteousness is something that the Lord gives us as a gift because of our relationship with Him and "works" is birthed out of our relationship with Him; "we don't do good to get saved, but rather we do good 'because' we are saved." The righteousness spoken of in scripture is about being in right standing with God. This brings about all of the promises of God because the promises are made to God's people. What part does its armor play? Our faith brings about righteousness; just as Abraham believed God; in spite of his physical limitations, he believed and his belief granted him God's righteousness.

Righteousness and faith go hand in hand. The righteousness of God is covering our hearts. In other words, the righteousness of God (His character and attributes) is covering our hearts, everything that is right, according to the Word of God has our hearts covered and protected; and when this is the case, nothing that the enemy brings our way can get into our heart (influence us to do his deeds). Remember now, it is imperative that we are steadfast in walking in righteousness because this is our protection in this battle we are in, and entering in, uncertain and afraid spells sure defeat; however, when we are in right standing with God, nothing is standing in the way of this relationship, thus we have nothing to fear because perfect love casts out fear, *"...There is no fear in love but perfect love casts out fear.* (1 John 4:18 NKJV); God is Love.

Because sin separates us from God, it is imperative that we are no longer living a life of perpetual, habitual sin (unrighteousness); which is displeasing to God. We must always, at all times, be sure that we are living a life that is constantly ready to repent of any sin that we have allowed to infiltrate our lives; like David, though he sinned by committing adultery with Bathsheba and then was responsible for the death of her husband Uriah, he was quick to repent and accept the consequences for his actions. To live a life like this simply means to walk in the way of God, not the world; living a life of repentance ensures that we will stay in the right relationship with God. The only way we can truly live this type of lifestyle is to *"...love not the world..."* One thing the enemy would try to have us believe is that when we sin, we must hide from God; however, running to God and not from Him, is the only way we can be assured of receiving deliverance; without the power of the

Holy Spirit, there is no way possible that we can consciously agree with God about our sin and turn away from it *"...not by might, not by power but by my Spirit says the Lord..."* (Zechariah 4:6 NKJV). We must always remember that God knew we would need His forgiveness and this is why He provided a way for us to remain in right standing with Him; by sending His only Son, *"For God sent not His Son into the world to condemn the world; but that the world through Him might be saved..."* (John 3:17 NKJV). As Believers, we can never forget that the privilege of deliverance is ours. He made it possible for us to run *to* Him after we sin and not away *from* Him. Satan will continue to accuse us and keep us burdened down with the weight of sin every time that we mess up. *"...Now is come salvation, and strength, and the kingdom of our God, and the power of his Christ: for the accuser of our brethren is cast down, which accused them before our God day and night..."* (Revelation 12:10 NKJV). We have got to remember what the Bible says concerning condemnation: *"Therefore, there is now no condemnation to those who are in Christ Jesus..."* (Romans 8:1 NKJV). This is a prime example of utilizing the armor we are instructed to "put on." When Satan tempted Jesus in the desert, Jesus responded with the Word of God; Jesus is our example, we also are to use the Word of God against satan, the enemy of our souls. Because he (satan) knows that when we know the Word of God, we are a force to be reckoned with, he attempts to distract us from becoming familiar with it and gaining a real understanding of it.

Take a moment to visualize this armored soldier once again. One who is covered in the armor. The armor is made of metal. The breastplate is made of something so strong that no arrow, bullet, dart, or any other type of harmful object can penetrate it. That's how God wants our righteousness. Unpenetratable! That's what Abraham had! No matter what, his faith could not be penetrated – thus showing his belief in God and it obviously pleased God! Not with our works, talents, gifts, or anything else in which we take pride. Faith is the only thing that will make a smile come to the face of God. – Find favor with Him! It's time to stop seeking the favor of the world and begin to seek the favor of the Lord! God's righteousness – All this is right! *"You love righteousness and hate wickedness; therefore God, your God has set you above your companions"* (Psalm 45:7 NKJV). There is a stark contrast because the world calls evil good and good evil but according to the Word of God, this is a dangerous place to be. *"Woe to those who call evil good and good evil..."* (Isaiah 20 NKJV). Here's the part we need to be sure of that we have a good covering over our heart and other vital organs. Whatever is in the heart affects and infects the rest of the body. Let's switch gears here for a moment and imagine a person who contracts an infection of some kind and it attacks the heart, that person normally ends up in the hospital in a very serious state, and sometimes even dies. The heart is the wellspring of life and therefore, we are to guard it with all diligence. *"Above all else, guard your heart, for it is the wellspring of life"* (Proverbs 4:23 NKJV). Therefore, if we have on the breastplate or rather, our armor which is meant to protect the very essence of our physical body from the attack of the enemy then we do well. We must never forget that we are in an ongoing battle; just as if we are going off to war and being sent home months later. This battle that we are in is a daily, unending war. So now, where is the breastplate that is protecting us spiritually?

Where is this righteousness that is protecting us? Remember now, righteousness is covering our heart. Jesus said that whatever is in our heart will come out of our mouth *"...out of the overflow of the heart the mouth speaks"* (Matthew 12:34 NKJV). What's inside *will* come out. Since it means being in right standing with God, we can begin to understand why this is also a vital part of the armor. If we don't know that we are in right standing with God, then we will be unsure in our convictions and will begin to believe every lie of the enemy when he tries to make us believe that we are unworthy, useless, etc..., etc... because of the things that we've done in the past. Now, here's the tricky part; as far as us being in right standing with God. If we are in right standing with God then we will begin to see things as He sees them. It's a process but one we need to embrace. John says *"If we claim to have fellowship with Him yet walk in the darkness, we lie and do not live by the truth"* (1 John 1:6 NKJV). The only way that we will know God and His Word is to saturate ourselves in His Word; making it an integral part of our daily life, we must become so familiar with it that we recognize the attacks of the enemy immediately. We need to be able to recognize counterfeit when we see them. Some time ago, I read an article explaining that the way the FBI trains its agents to recognize counterfeit bills is to first introduce them to the real thing; every intricate detail of the real bill is studied over and over again and then the counterfeit is introduced and immediately recognized and because the agent has "intimate" knowledge of the real thing; immediately viewing the counterfeit, it is recognized as such. Now, if we become so intimate with God and His Word, then when the counterfeit, the lies of the enemy comes along, the "red flag" will be raised and we won't fall for the tricks of the enemy of our soul.

Feet Shod with the Preparation of the Gospel of Peace

Let's look at the feet; they take us where we need or want to go, the feet allow us to step freely and without fear while we turn our full attention to the battle at hand. They aid in our movement and defense. The feet propel us onward to proclaim the true peace, which is available in Jesus. We are admonished to *"go ye into all the world…"* We must be prepared to follow the Lord at all times, no matter what.

Knowing the gospel enables us to have the peace of God because He is our peace. Imagine putting feet on the peace that we have from knowing Christ. Scripture says *"how beautiful are the feet of them that preach the gospel…"* (Romans 10:15 NKJV). There will be so much peace that we will literally be beautiful to behold; something that cannot be explained. One that will draw people to us without them even knowing *why* they are drawn to us. Then after they are drawn to us, we can give them the great news of the Gospel. If the enemy can keep us from knowing and spreading this peace, his kingdom is advanced even more in the earth realm. But if we know this peace then *and begin to* spread it, the efforts of the enemy become more and more frustrating to him. His main goal is to have us in a perpetual state of confusion and frustration which ultimately leads to defeat. However, when we have the peace of God activated in our lives, there is absolutely nothing that the enemy of our souls can send our way, not a flaming arrow, a dart, or an accusation that can penetrate the fortress of peace that surrounds us. As God's children, we have this confidence because we can read in scripture where God has given His angels charge over us lest we should stumble along the way. *"He who dwells in the secret place of the Most High shall abide under the shadow of the Almighty. I will say of the Lord, He is my refuge and my fortress My God, in Him I will trust. Surely He shall deliver you from the snare of the fowler and from the perilous pestilence. He shall cover you with His feathers and under His wings you shall take refuge; His truth shall be your shield and buckler. You shall not be afraid of the terror by night, nor of the arrow that flies by day. Nor of the pestilence that walks in darkness, nor of the destruction that lays waste at noonday. A thousand may fall at your side, and ten thousand at your right hand; but it shall not come near you. Only with your eyes shall you look, and see the reward of the wicked. Because you have made the Lord, who is my refuge, even the Most High your dwelling place, no evil will befall you in all your ways. In their hands they shall bear you up, lest you dash your foot against a stone..."* (Psalm 91 KJV)

The reason the enemy wants us ignorant to the peace of God is because he knows that once we are walking in this confidence, we will be able to stand against him unwaveringly. *"...He who sits in the heavens shall laugh..."* (Psalm 2:4 NKJV). Once we really grab ahold of and have a full understanding, we are further on our way to becoming fully equipped and be able to do some serious damage to Satan and his kingdom of darkness. Satan is truly is afraid of a fully armored soldier, one of *God's* fully armored soldiers. So now, not only are angels there to protect us but to also comfort us. One of the commands that Jesus left was *"...go therefore and make disciples..."* (Matthew 28:19 NKJV). That involves preaching the good news of the gospel, we are told to make disciples of all nations. Sometimes, mistakenly the popular thinking in the body of Christ is that only a person who serves in the pulpit is supposed to fulfill this command. But it's quite the contrary, every Believer who clothes themselves with the title of "Christian" has this responsibility. The bible says that all believers have the "ministry of reconciliation" *"...Now, all things are of God, who has reconciled us to Himself, through Jesus Christ, and has given us the ministry of reconciliation, that is, that God was in Christ reconciling the world to Himself, not imputing their trespasses to them, and has committed to us the word of reconciliation..."* (2 Corinthians 5:18-19 NKJV).

Shield of Faith

"...above all, taking the shield of faith with which you will be able to quench all the fiery darts of the wicked one." (Eph 6:16 NKJV)

Faith - Believing that everything will work out the way that God intends for it to, even if it is not what I believed or hoped for (Heb 11:1).

Shield - Protection, deflection

"Knowing" and "Believing" in Christ and everything about Him will influence the way that we live this life. Our faith determines how we face trials, and circumstances; if our faith is strong then when circumstances happen (and they surely will) we will face them with peace because we'll remind ourselves *"He did it before and He'll do it again; He brought me through before and He'll do it again. I can trust Him to bring me through even if the outcome is different than what I'm hoping for.* We can have faith because before Jesus left to be crucified He told His disciple *"...these things I've spoken to you that in Me you might have peace. In the world you will have tribulation but be of good cheer, I have overcome the world"* (John 16:33 NKJV)

Envision a shield; what is its purpose? Its purpose is to cover or protect. Since we know that God highly values "faith" then we will understand that when the "shield of faith" is covering us then we are covered from any and everything that the enemy or the world can send our way. The shield of faith will deflect every bad thing that would come our way in order to stop or hinder us from knowing God and walking in the things of God; all things good.

When we look at the book of Hebrews chapter 11 (often referred to as "the chapter of faith") we see how the lives of the men of old played out simply based on their faith. How we ought to respond to God and His commands while walking in faith.

The scripture tells us *"By faith we understand that the worlds were framed by the Word of God, so that the things which are seen were not made of things which are visible"* (Hebrews 11:4 NKJV).

By faith, *"Abel offered God a more excellent sacrifice than Cain, through which he obtained witness that he was righteous, God testifying of his gifts; and through it he being dead still speaks…"* (Hebrews 11:4 NKJV) God was so pleased with Abel's offerings that the account of his life reserved a place in God's holy writ and is one of the examples as to how we the "New Testament Believer" should govern our lives concerning our offerings unto God. His example did not die when he did.

By faith, *"Enoch was taken away so that he did not see death and was not found because God had taken him, for before he was taken he had this testimony, that he pleased God. But without faith it is impossible to please Him, for he who comes to God must believe that He is, and that He is a rewarder of those who diligently seek Him"* (Hebrews 4:5 NKJV) By contrast of other men of old with the exception of Elijah, Enoch simply "was not" meaning that he did not "taste" death. The bible tells us that Enoch "walked with God" meaning that he faithfully walked closely with God; now one can deduce that Enoch was truly pleasing to God. The scripture tells us that *"…So all the days of Enoch were three hundred and sixty-five years. And Enoch walked with God; and he was not, for God took him…"* (Genesis 5:23-24 NKJV). So we see that Enoch's life was totally dedicated to God, the statement *"...walked with God..."* intimates that there was a closeness like none other between the two. In order for one to walk in such intimacy with God, there *must* be unusual faith involved. Then further, the fact that Enoch simply 'was not' implies that his relationship with God was such that the intimacy was too great for this natural world to contain or comprehend. So yes, Enoch pleased God! Enoch's *faith* pleased God! Enoch was rewarded tremendously and his reward was birthed out of his relationship *with* God! So we see firsthand, an example of a person who truly had the "shield" of faith protecting his life.

Helmet of Salvation

Since the mind is the place where the spiritual battle takes place, it is attacked the most fierce with satan's lies. He attempts to get us to doubt God and His saving work and grace for us. Satan knows that without faith there is absolutely no way that we can please God, so he attempts to get us out of fellowship *with* God. The helmet protects our minds from doubting the truth of God's Word as well as His saving work for us. The Helmet of Salvation is a precise understanding and working knowledge of the Word of God (Bible). The only way this can be achieved is by using what the Lord reveals to us through His methods. We must be willing to open ourselves up to the hand of the Lord, He is the only one that can and will lead us into the deep understanding of His Word and Truth. The Lenemy would love to deceive us as he did Adam and Eve in the Garden but we must guard against his tricks and deceit at all times. The helmet protects the head – there is an old adage, *"cut off the head and the rest of the body will die"* – this is why the attacks of the enemy in this area are so effective; He doesn't pull any punches. Since he is as effective as he is, we must likewise be committed to protecting ourselves diligently. That is why it is so important that we protect our heads with the Helmet of Salvation. Remember how the little Shepard boy David slew the giant Goliath? Well, he went straight for the head, and IMMEDIATELY Goliath was down and out. Because anything without a head cannot survive. Scripture tells us that we will "live and not die." Now, all we have to do is *believe* this. The Lord has His hand upon us at all times but we must only believe this.

As for us, the "Helmet of Salvation" is vital for survival (spiritual survival that is); we can thwart the enemy's attacks against us by activating our assurance of salvation. When we are sure of our salvation, then we can stay in the fight without becoming overwhelmed with fear or confusion which is in the enemy's arsenal of weapons against us. The reason that he uses these two together is that if he can get us to doubt that God loves us and can be trusted then half the battle against us has been won. Jesus said, *"Do not be afraid of those who kill the body but cannot kill the soul. Rather, be afraid of the One who can destroy both soul and body in hell"* (Matthew 10:28 NKJV). The idea of spending blissful eternity with God is one that comforts the Believer in our walk while here on this earth; this idea is a driving force behind us being able to endure whatever may come our way while here on earth. Scripture even proves this in speaking of Jesus on His way to the cross; scripture says *"...let us lay aside every weight, and the sin which so easily ensnares us and let us run with endurance the race that is set before us, looking unto Jesus, the author and finisher of our faith, who for the joy set before Him endured the cross, despising the shame, and has sat down at the right hand of the throne of God..."* (Hebrew 12:1-2) NKJV. Now if Jesus being fully human and fully God who at one point cried out to God in the Garden of Gethsemane *"...if it were possible let this cup pass from me; Nevertheless not My will but Yours..."* (Matthew 26:39 NKJV) could go forward and submit His will to the Father and complete the task at hand (going to the Cross), be strengthened by the thought of what lay beyond the Cross (eternity with the Father). Then because He is our example so we too, can walk here on this earth, and not be moved by the enemy because we also know that there is something so great in our future (eternity with Jesus); this is the very reason the enemy attempts to "get in our head" with his many lies. We have the responsibility of making sure that he does not cause us to remove our "helmet of salvation." This is so precious to us the Believer and we *must* protect it at all costs. He knows that the salvation that lies ahead for us, he no longer has any hold on us. Many of God's children do not know this truth and do not live as if they know it and the enemy knows this and that's why he continues attempts to keep them ignorant of the fact. But we have the responsibility of keeping our helmets buckled tightly so that when he sends his fiery darts flying in our direction they do not find a landing place in our minds. This weapon of "Helmet of Salvation" is what allows us to destroy and cast down everything the enemy sends our way. *"…casting down arguments (imaginations) and every high thing that exalts itself against the knowledge of God, bringing every thought into captivity to the obedience of Christ…"* (2 Corinthians 10:5 NKJV). Some of the actions that we the Believer can take against the enemy are by:

Renewing the mind

We are told to renew our mind by allowing only God's truth to destroy anything that is contrary to God's Word... *"...do not be conformed to this world, but be transformed by the renewing of your mind that you may prove what is that good and acceptable and perfect will of God..."* (Romans 12:1-2 NKJV) In other words, replace all our old ways of thinking, get rid of all *"stinkin' thinkin'"* that used to govern our walk and instead replace it with God's truth concerning every area of our lives. Continually cast down any and all doubts concerning circumstances in our lives. *Circumstances* can sometimes cause us to doubt God's sovereignty in our lives; they will sometimes cause us to doubt God's love. However, we must counter that with His truth; even if the circumstances seem to say otherwise, we must activate our faith that says *"In spite of what it looks like, God has promised that He will never leave or forsake me"* Always activate our faith in the face of trials because we know this pleases God. (Hebrews 11:6). Constantly speaking the Word helps us in this process. We must always remind ourselves that a glorious eternity awaits us and that regardless of what a situation appears to be, there's always hope! As we walk in God's truth on a daily basis we are protected against the onslaught of the enemy with his suggestions, desires, traps that he has planned for us on a daily basis. We must make a conscious decision to protect and guard our mind against everything that he will send to assault our senses; choose to obey scripture which says *"Be anxious for nothing, but in everything by prayer and supplication, with thanksgiving let your requests be made known to God..."* and receive His peace that He promises *"...the peace of God, which surpasses all understanding, will guard your hearts and minds through Christ Jesus..."* (Philippians 4:6-7 NKJV). And then let God govern our thoughts *"...whatever things are true, whatever things are noble, whatever things are just, whatever things are pure, whatever things are lovely, whatever things are of good report, if there is any virtue and if there is anything praiseworthy-meditate on these things..."* (Philippians 4:8 NKJV). We must inundate our thoughts with things of God on a second by second, minute by minute, hour by hour basis daily. This is what will protect us against ALL the attacks of the wicked one.

Sword of the Spirit (Word of God)

Put on *"the Sword of the Spirit, which is the Word of God."* (Ephesians 6:17) - The sword is the only weapon of offense in the armor, but it is also a tool for defense. Strongholds, arguments, and thoughts are all weapons the enemy uses against us. With the Sword of the Spirit, God's word, the people are equipped to deal with them all. We need to trust in the truth of God's Word. Have confidence in the value of God's word. Get a hunger and desire for God's Word. Just as the soldier needed to be trained in the use of the Sword, we the Believer need to be trained in the use of the Sword of the Spirit, when used correctly it will protect us spiritually just as a sword in the natural protected the soldier during battle. We must never forget that we are in a spiritual battle with a formidable enemy but we are not to fear him! Just as it was imperative that the soldier know how to handle and use the sword correctly, we too must be trained to know how to use our Sword of the Spirit correctly in order to get the maximum use out of it; then and only then can it be used to demolish everything that the enemy is assaulting us with. The purpose of the Sword of the Spirit is to make us a strong soldier, able to counterattack and fight this enemy of ours; we must be spiritually strong and mature in order to successfully fight in this battle. If we allow ourselves to become mature then we will be effective in standing against the enemy of our souls.

The only sure-fire way that we will effectively utilize the Sword of the Spirit is by being familiar with it; reading, studying on a daily basis. Unfortunately, many people think that the reading and studying of the Word of God is only for the preacher, pastor, teacher but we know this is not true because everyone is to *"study to show yourself approved..."* (2 Timothy 2:15 NKJV); Also Joshua 1:8 is an admonishment for us to "Meditate on the 'book of the law' day and night, and after doing this, we will be prosperous in our walk with the Lord. The bible *"...is profitable for doctrine, for reproof, for correction, for instruction in righteousness..."* (2 Timothy 3:16 NKJV).

We must always be on the defensive against the devil understanding that the only way this is possible is by using the Sword of the Spirit (Word of God; Bible) which is our defensive weapon. We see from Scripture that we must be vigilant because he (the enemy) is roaming the earth *"seeking whom he may devour"* and anytime we let our guard down, there is no doubt about it, we *will* be devoured *"...Be self-controlled and alert. Your enemy the devil prowls around like a roaring lion looking for someone to devour..."* (1 Peter 5:8 NKJV). Once again, this has been going on since the beginning of time; when Cain became angry with his brother Abel, God even admonished him saying *"...'Why are you angry? And why has your countenance fallen? If you do well, will you not be accepted? And if you do not do well, sin lies at the door. And its desire is for you, but you should rule over it..."* (Genesis 4:6-7 NKJV). Now, though we must never, ever let our guard down; this does not mean should become paranoid and start living in a state of perpetual fear but, always be on the alert for the attacks of the enemy. Not in a timid, afraid manner but always ready to retaliate at the first sign of trouble from the enemy of our souls. *"Be sober, be vigilant; because your adversary the devil walks about like a roaring lion, seeking whom he may devour. Resist him....* (1 Peter 5:8-9a NKJV). Understanding that when striking in a defensive manner, it must be done with precise, deliberate movements so that the blows land with brutal strikes, yes this may sound like a vicious attack and in reality it is. The devil isn't playing around and we shouldn't either! He has a deep, dark hatred for anything pertaining to God, especially the offspring, the children of God.

PRAYING Always (1 Thessalonians 5:17)

"Praying always with all prayer and supplication in the Spirit, being watchful to this end with all perseverance and supplication for all the saints" (Ephesians 6:18)

Prayer!! Hallelujah for Prayer! Our line of communication straight to the Throne of God! Though many people dread the thought of prayer simply because they are looking at it as something boring to be endured; not realizing that this is truly a privilege and an honor; scripture tells us *"let us then approach the throne of Grace with confidence, so that we may receive mercy and find grace to help us in our time of need."* (Hebrews 4:16 NKJV). We can run right to the feet of Jesus; not only are we meant to, but we are also expected to. Have you ever just began to speak to the Lord and waited for His response? That is exactly what He desires and expects from us. Though He knows all of our wants and needs, He is still waiting for us to tell Him; cast all of our burdens upon Him. *"Pray without ceasing"* (Thessalonians 5:17 NKJV). The author Paul here is not talking about just talking non-stop, he is rather talking about an attitude of "God-consciousness" and surrendering on a daily basis. As we go about our daily life we are to live being aware that God is with us constantly and He should always be in the forefront of our minds; actively involved and we should engage Him in every thought and action. As the enemy attempts to assault our mind and thoughts with worry, anger, fear then we are to actively engage God, remembering that we are to turn every thought to make it a matter of prayer. He is very humorous. I remember one time as I woke up and began to speak to Him I said *"Lord, do you know what I'm thinking?"*

and lo and behold the Holy Spirit responded *"Yes, but tell me anyway"* Isn't it awesome that this is the kind of God that we serve. The Lord wants us to know Him on a personal level not just coming to Him with our wish list or list of problems, He wants fellowship, we were created for His good pleasure. *"...for You created all things, and by Your will they exist and were created"* (Revelation 4:11 NKJV).

Jesus is to be our example and one of the most profound examples is what He did early in the morning before He even made any decisions He went away to a solitary place and prayed, just spent time with Him and the Father. *"And in the morning, rising up a great while before day, He went out, and departed into a solitary place, and there prayed"* (Mark 1:35). Also, when He was facing the biggest challenge of His life here on earth, He disappeared to the Garden of Gethsemane to talk to God. *"...and said to the disciples, 'sit here while I go and pray over there."* (Matthew 26:36 NKJV) *"And He went a little farther and fell on His face, and prayed, saying 'O My Father, if it is possible, let this cup pass from Me; nevertheless, not as I will but as You will...*(Matthew 26:39 NKJV). After Jesus submitted His will, even though He knew His thoughts were already known He did not hesitate to express His innermost thoughts to God. However, He had to rebuke His own disciples for falling asleep while He was out doing what we are commanded to do *(pray without ceasing)*; though they walked with Him daily they still fell short of what was expected of them. But Jesus didn't get angry with them, He just told them what it was that they needed in order to make it through life down here on earth. *"Watch and pray, that ye enter not into temptation: the Spirit indeed is willing, but the flesh is weak..."* (Matthew 26:41

NKJV). The key is a personal relationship with the Father! When the enemy no longer has us bound by fear, then the battle is won. I will be forever grateful to the Lord for the day that the boldness of the Holy Spirit rose up in me and as this tormenting, evil spirit tried to attack me as it had so many times before, I was able to face it and with confidence say these very words, *"I am not afraid of you – in the name of Jesus, I command you to flee"* after that encounter, he tried once again and out of habit, I almost became afraid, however; immediately, the Holy Spirit reminded me that I had the victory and I was able to say once again with full confidence in the Lord *"you do not scare me, I am no longer afraid of you – in the name of Jesus, I command you to flee."* God is so faithful to all of us as His children, we just must only believe. Prayer for us should be compared to breathing, it should be a normal response in our everyday life, the question posed to the Believer should not be *"How often do you pray"* but rather *"How often do you not pray?"* It should be commonplace to always have a prayer in our heart; subconsciously communing with God; always aware of His presence in our daily lives. We should live a life that is constantly, persistently talking to God; prayers should be an essential part of our daily lives with a spirit of humility and dependence on God.

So now, are you "Suited and Ready for Battle?!

About the Author

Karen D. Carver-Prater the fourth of six children is also the author of *"Dancing While in The Valley"*, she is a lover of a good televised documentary, swimming, crafting, reading, and long afternoon strolls. When she is not doing the aforementioned, she's likely busy with toiling in the ministry "Full Armored Ministries" of which she is the Founder/Senior Pastor, or you can find her working and building her brand "Nothin' but BLING!!!" of which she is the Owner/Operator.

Author Karen hails from Niagara Falls, N.Y. A self-described "Army Brat", she has lived over much of the United States. The mother of two adult children, Natasha and Terrell Washington and "Nana" to two, Ricardo (AKA Ricky) and Jeremiah.

Author Karen, after having spent over 25 years in Huntsville, AL now resides in Concord, NC with her husband Steven and two dogs' "Cookie" and "Bandit." Thank you for your purchase and it is our prayer that you will be fully armored after reading each page of this book.

To contact Author Karen, please forward all inquiries to 757-912-7014 or Praterpearl@yahoo.com

www.ingramcontent.com/pod-product-compliance
Lightning Source LLC
Chambersburg PA
CBHW051707090426
42736CB00013B/2588